RIPLEY's DINOSAURS

Believe It or Not!®

RIPLEY
PUBLISHING

a Jim Pattison Company

Written by Rupert Matthews
Consultant Steve Parker

PUBLISHING

Publisher Anne Marshall

Editorial Director Rebecca Miles
Project Editor Lisa Regan
Editor Rosie Alexander
Assistant Editor Charlotte Howell
Picture Researchers James Proud, Charlotte Howell
Proofreader Judy Barratt
Indexer Hilary Bird

Art Director Sam South
Senior Designer Michelle Foster
Design Rocket Design (East Anglia) Ltd
Reprographics Juice Creative Ltd

www.ripleybooks.com

ISBN 978-1-893951-80-8
10 9 8 7 6 5 4 3 2

For information regarding permission, write to
VP Intellectual Property, Ripley Entertainment Inc., Suite 188, 7576 Kingspointe Parkway, Orlando, Florida 32819
email: publishing@ripleys.com
Library of Congress Cataloging-in-Publication Data
Matthews, Rupert.
    Twists dinosaurs / [written by Rupert Matthews].
            p. cm. -- (Ripley's believe it or not!)
    Includes index.
     ISBN 978-1-893951-80-8
    1. Dinosaurs--Miscellanea--Juvenile literature. 2. Dinosaurs--Extinction--Juvenile literature. I. Title
QE861.5.M374 2010
    567.9--dc22
                              2010020093

Manufactured in China
In December/2010 by RR Donnelley
2nd Printing

PUBLISHER'S NOTE
While every effort has been made to verify the accuracy of the entries in this book, the Publishers cannot be held responsible for any errors contained in the work. They would be glad to receive any information from readers.

WARNING
Some of the stunts and activities in this book are undertaken by experts and should not be attempted by anyone without adequate training and supervision.

CONTENTS

TWISTS

PAGE 26

PAGE 12

DINOSAUR DAYS

PREHISTORIC PLANET

Could you have survived living with the dinosaurs? Would you have managed to escape the terrifying teeth of the *Tyrannosaurus*, or avoid the slashing claws of a *Velociraptor*? Even if you did, would you have been happy eating moss or ferns in this strange and bizarre place? Or could you have captured a baby dinosaur—and then roasted it for your supper? In this book you will learn all you need to know about the world of the dinosaurs.

WHAT'S INSIDE YOUR BOOK?

Millions of years ago the world was a very different place. Dinosaurs stalked the Earth, other reptiles flew in the skies and swam in the seas, and the largest mammal around was the size of a badger.

Do the twist

This book is packed with cool pictures and awesome facts. It will teach you amazing things about dinosaurs, but like all Twists books, it shines a spotlight on things that are unbelievable but true. Turn the pages and find out more...

Tyrannosaurus

Spinosaurus

20

THE GREAT DEATH

Sixty-five million years ago, all the dinosaurs died out, along with many marine reptiles, flying reptiles, and other types of animal. However, a few creatures survived, including lizards, birds, insects, and our own ancestors—the early mammals. Which is just as well for us!

TWISTS

BIG WORD ALERT

PALEOICHNOLOGIST

A scientist who studies fossils of things left behind by animals, such as footprints and nests.

Found a new word? Big word alerts will explain it for you.

A pterosaur becomes lunch!

These books are all about "Believe It or Not!"—amazing facts, feats, and things that will make you go "Wow!"

PRIZE FIGHTERS

...ver Struggles

...ke a ringside seat ...is fight of the era. ...ging toward each ...t top speed, a pair ...ratops clash with ...nding "thwack." ...ck together, the ...brates, as each ...trong shoulder ...try to wrestle ...ackward into ...les between ...s would have ...rifying.

...eat-eating ...ed to fight. ...rs had to ...urs of the ...r territory, ...ome used ...feathers ...others had ...se in their ...contest ...njury, but ...uld have ...ghts.

YEE-HAA!

Whip crack away

Seismosaurus and other sauropods had enormously long, whip-like tails that were controlled by powerful muscles. They could have used these tails to lash each other into defeat. Sauropods may also have used their necks to swing their heads and butt each other, in a similar way to giraffes today.

twist it!

Torosaurus had the largest frilled dinosaur skull, which was more than 8 feet long.

Daspletosaurus was a slightly smaller relative of Tyrannosaurus that had a gaping mouth filled with huge sharp-ripped teeth. In battles, these dinosaurs would try to bite each other's faces, often inflicting deep gashes, which have been found on some fossils.

One family of dinosaurs had enormously thick bony domes on top of their skulls that were up to an incredible 8 inches thick. The family was given the name of pachycephalosaurs, which means "thick-headed-reptiles."

COME HERE AND SAY THAT!

Triceratops means "three-horned face."

Triceratops had no front teeth, so its mouth looked like a turtle's beak.

Ripley's Believe It or Not!

WHAT'S THE POINT?

Stegosaur tails all had a tip armed with long, sharp spikes called a "thagomizer." This unusual name was originally part of a joke in a 1982 cartoon by Gary Larson in which an unfortunate caveman called Thag has been killed by such a weapon. It is now used as an official term by paleontologists worldwide!

One of the most recognizable of all the dinosaurs, Triceratops was a plant-eating whopper that stood up to 10 feet tall and 30 feet in length. Its enormous skull could be one third the length of its body and its famous horns were probably used in mating rituals as well as for defense.

Don't forget to look out for the "twist it!" column on some pages. Twist the book to find out more fascinating facts about dinosaurs.

Learn fab fast facts to go with the cool pictures.

Go to page 44 for more facts about the crazy creatures in this book

DINOSAUR BASICS

Striding across the ground, some of the largest, most incredible animals ever to walk the Earth made the ground shake with every thundering footstep. For over 160 million years, the dinosaurs were one of the most successful groups of animals our planet had ever seen... then they vanished.

The dinosaurs were a huge group of reptiles that lived all over the world. There were more than 700 different types of dinosaur. Some were enormous, but others were tiny. Many were slow and clumsy, a lot were fast and agile. Dinosaurs included several types of animal that looked utterly bizarre, and some that might not look unusual if they were alive today.

TOTAL TYRANNOSAURUS

> Tyrannosaurus had very short arms with powerful two-clawed fingers. These were probably used to seize prey, but were too short to reach its mouth.

> The closest living relative to Tyrannosaurus is the plain old chicken!

> Tyrannosaurus could eat up to 500 pounds of meat in one sitting—that's equivalent to 2,000 burgers!

DINO FACTS

- The word "dinosaur" means "terrible lizard."

- The tallest dinosaurs were over 50 feet in height—that's as high as a five-story building—and weighed as much as ten elephants.

- The smallest dinosaurs were about the size of a chicken.

- The fastest dinosaurs could run at about 45 mph—that's faster than a racehorse.

HOW TO SPOT A DINOSAUR

Dinosaurs shared the following features, which helped to make them undisputed rulers of the Earth:

- A long tail for balance that made it easier for them to run quickly.

- Straight legs that tucked underneath their bodies, making moving more energy efficient.

- A prong on the astragalus (a bone in the ankle) that allowed for the attachment of strong tendons to aid agile movement.

- A bulge on the humerus (a bone in the upper leg) that allowed for powerful muscles to be attached to aid fast running.

EYE SOCKET

UPPER JAW

NOSTRIL

LOWER JAW

FRONT CLAWS

REAR CLAWS

TAIL

RIBS

UPPER LEG

FOOT

WATCH OUT!

STUDYING DINOSAURS

Scientists studying dinosaurs are constantly making new discoveries about these amazing creatures. Only recently they concluded that birds probably evolved from one dinosaur group, and that several groups of dinosaurs had feathers!

Looking at fossils can be a confusing business, especially as most dinosaur fossils found are not complete. But, as more and more fossils are unearthed, we learn more about dinosaurs and the world in which they lived. These incredible creatures were around for such a long time that some evolved and others became extinct millions of years apart.

BIG WORD ALERT

MESOZOIC ERA
The time in which the dinosaurs lived, made up of the Triassic, Jurassic, and Cretaceous Periods.

Pterosaur
Dinosaurs lived only on land, but they shared their world with flying reptiles called pterosaurs (see page 38) and several groups of water-dwelling reptiles (see page 40).

Diplodocus
This was one of the sauropod group of dinosaurs (see page 14). All sauropods were four-legged plant-eating giants and many had long whip-like tails.

The Time Lords

First signs of life 3.5 bya

First dinosaur 230 mya

First pterosaurs 220 mya

Diplodocus 155 mya

Stegosaurus 150 mya

Triassic period	Jurassic period

8

251 mya

bya = billion years ago
mya = million years ago

200 mya

145 mya

MESOZOIC ERA

HIP-HIP-ARRAY!

- All dinosaurs belonged to one of two groups, based on the shape of their hip bones. One group had hips shaped like those of a modern reptile. These are called lizard-hipped dinosaurs, or saurischians. The other group had hips shaped like those of a modern bird, and are called bird-hipped dinosaurs, or ornithischians.

- The bird-hipped dinosaurs were all plant-eaters. The lizard-hipped dinosaurs were divided into two further groups—theropods, who were all meat-eaters, and the sauropods, who were all plant-eaters with long necks and long tails.

- Surprisingly, many scientists believe that birds today are descended from the lizard-hipped theropods, not from bird-hipped dinosaurs as you might expect.

Lizard-hipped

Bird-hipped

Stegosaurus

Stegosaurus is famous for having a very small brain. Despite not being the brightest of dinosaurs, it was around for many millions of years.

Triceratops

Arriving on the scene just 3 million years before the dinosaurs' mass extinction, Triceratops is recognized by the shape of the horns and large bony frill on its head.

First flowers 125 mya

Triceratops 68 mya

People evolve

Cretaceous period

CENOZOIC ERA

65 mya

You are here

WHAT'S THE EVIDENCE?

The dinosaurs lived many millions of years ago. Not a single one is alive today, so there is no chance to study them in the wild or look at them in a zoo.

We know about dinosaurs only because scientists have found their remains buried in rocks. These remains are known as fossils and are usually the imprint of bones, teeth, and other hard parts of a dinosaur body. Muscles, organs, and other soft parts do not often get preserved as fossils. Scientists use the fossils to try to work out what the dinosaur looked like when it was alive. They study details on the dinosaur's bones to decide where its muscles, eyes, stomach, and other missing parts would have been.

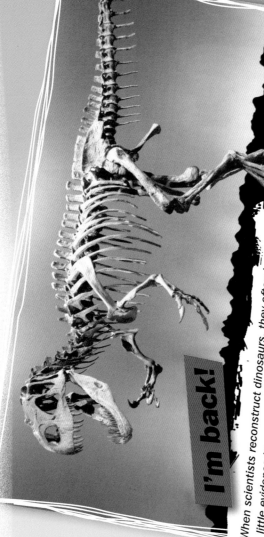

I'm back!

When scientists reconstruct dinosaurs, they often have very little evidence to work with, but meat-eating Afrovenator, here, was found as a single almost complete skeleton. The dinosaur was 30 feet long from its nose to the tip of its tail.

SAVING ITS SKIN

Dinosaur skin was often scaly, as indicated by this fossil from the hindquarters of a *Triceratops* that died 65 million years ago in Hell Creek, Montana. Fossils rarely record accurate color, so scientists in the past guessed that dinosaur skin was dark green or brown, like crocodile or alligator skin. More recently, they have changed their minds and now think dinosaurs may have come in a rainbow of colors—some green, some red, and some even sporting spots or stripes!

Believe It or Not!®

Bone home

Medicine Bone Cabin near Medicine Bow, Wyoming, is built completely from dinosaur bones. Thomas Boylan began collecting dinosaur bone fragments in 1916. By 1933, which he discarded a dig in 1916, from a nearby dinosaur dig he had gathered 5,796 bones, and from a lodge he decided to use to construct a then measuring 29 feet long and 19 feet wide—that's the length of a Stegosaurus.

HOW TO MAKE A FOSSIL

Take one newly dead dinosaur.

Leave for 1,000 years until its skeleton has been covered by deposits of mud or sand.

Allow layers of rocks, minerals, and even oceans to build up on top of the dinosaur, preserving its skeleton deep beneath the Earth's surface.

After 80 million more years the landscape changes and the rocks containing the dinosaur's fossilized remains are exposed once more.

Feathered friends

In 1997, Chinese scientists in Liaoning Province found the fossilized remains of a small hunting dinosaur named Caudipteryx. They were astonished to see that the dinosaur had been covered in feathers. This led many scientists to believe that birds evolved from dinosaurs.

What's in a name?

If scientists discover an entirely new type of dinosaur, they are allowed to give it a name. Most scientists use names from ancient Greek or Latin that describe a feature of the fossil, such as Triceratops, which means "three-horned face." Other scientists use the name of the person who place the fossil was found, the name of the person who found it, or even what the weather was like at the time!

Dig that

In 1909, scientist Earl Douglass discovered some dinosaur fossils near Jensen in Utah, USA. He began digging, and scientists haven't stopped since—they are still finding fossils there today. More than 10,000 dinosaur fossils have been discovered at this one site, which is now preserved as the Dinosaur National Monument.

SUCH A SOFTY

In 1981, an amateur paleontologist discovered this 113-million-year-old fossilized Scipionyx dinosaur in Italy. What makes it unique is that 85 percent of its body is intact, including its windpipe, muscles, intestines, and other internal organs.

PALEONTOLOGIST
A scientist who studies fossils, animals and plants.

BIG WORD ALERT

HOME SWEET HOME

DINOSAUR WORLD VIEW

BIG WORD ALERT

CONTINENT
Any of the world's main continuous areas of land, such as Africa or Asia.

The world the dinosaurs inhabited was very different from our own. Strange plants grew on the ground and bizarre creatures swam in the seas or flew in the skies. Even the continents were in different places.

During the Triassic period, dinosaurs inland coped with throat-drying desert zones, while, during the Jurassic period, they enjoyed a warm, wet climate. The Cretaceous period had both warm and cool times, and huge, shallow seas spread over the planet. Their warm waters evaporated and fell as heavy rain on land. Vast forests started to grow. Some plants and insects we see today existed back then and provided dinosaurs with a variety of foods, such as leafy ferns, pine trees, mushrooms, magnolias, dragonflies, and tasty termites.

Pangaea

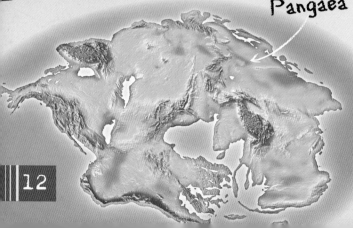

ONE WORLD

When the age of dinosaurs began, all the continents on Earth were joined together into a vast landmass that scientists call Pangaea, which means "all of earth." About 170 million years ago, Pangaea split in two, forming Laurasia and Gondwanaland. About 130 million years ago, Gondwanaland began to split up to form South America, India, Africa, Australia, and Antarctica. Laurasia divided about 50 million years ago into North America and Europe-Asia.

PHWOAR!

WHAT A STINK!

In Kawah Ijen, Indonesia, miners cover their mouths to protect against choking on sulfurous gas, as they pull stinking sulfur from a volcanic crater. The air dinosaurs breathed often must have been just as bad. Volcanic eruptions during the Mesozoic era pumped out huge quantities of sulfur and other evil-smelling gases. In wet areas, swamps containing rotting vegetation would have stunk. And don't even think about the terrible-smelling breath of the carnivorous dinosaurs, with rotten meat festering in their teeth.

Some of today's flora and fauna would have been known to the dinosaurs.

MAGNOLIA

HORSETAIL FERN

CYCAD

twist it!

CALLING PLANET EARTH

The very first flowering plants appeared about 125 million years ago in eastern Asia, during the early Cretaceous period. Some 25 million years later, flowering plants suddenly spread right across the world and took over from earlier types of plants.

The climate of the world was at its hottest about 110 million years ago, when it was around 10°F warmer than it is today.

In the later Cretaceous Period vast volcanic eruptions spurted molten rock across India. An area of land about 600,000 square miles was covered in lava about 1¼ miles thick.

Where did you come from?

When fossils of the same animal are found on different continents it suggests that those continents were once joined together. This is because large land animals couldn't get across oceans and only traveled around by walking.

Fossils of the crocodile-like reptile Uberabasuchus—seen here having a dinosaur for dinner—have been found in South America, Africa, and Madagascar, suggesting how these landmasses were joined together about 100 million years ago.

GNAAAAAR

HOW BIG?

SUPER SAUROPODS

Imagine if the sauropods—the biggest of all the dinosaurs—roamed our streets today. These gentle giants would be able to peer into windows five floors up and crush cars as if they were toys. They were the largest animals that have ever walked the Earth.

Argentinosaurus
About 100 feet long (head to tail)
Weighed a colossal 88 tons

Mamenchisaurus
About 43 feet long
Had a neck that was
half its total body length

Brachiosaurus
About 80 feet long
Could raise its neck 2–3 times
higher than a giraffe

The sauropods were a group of plant-eating dinosaurs that had long necks and long tails. They had small mouths, so they had to eat almost continuously to consume enough food. They couldn't chew, so they had huge stomachs and intestines—filling most of their body—to process the leaves and twigs on which they fed. Sauropods first appeared about 200 million years ago and by 150 million years ago were the most important types of plant-eating dinosaurs.

Sauropods swallowed stones and pebbles that remained in their stomachs. As the stomach muscles churned the food about, the stones pummeled the leaves and twigs to a mushy liquid that could be more easily digested in their huge intestines.

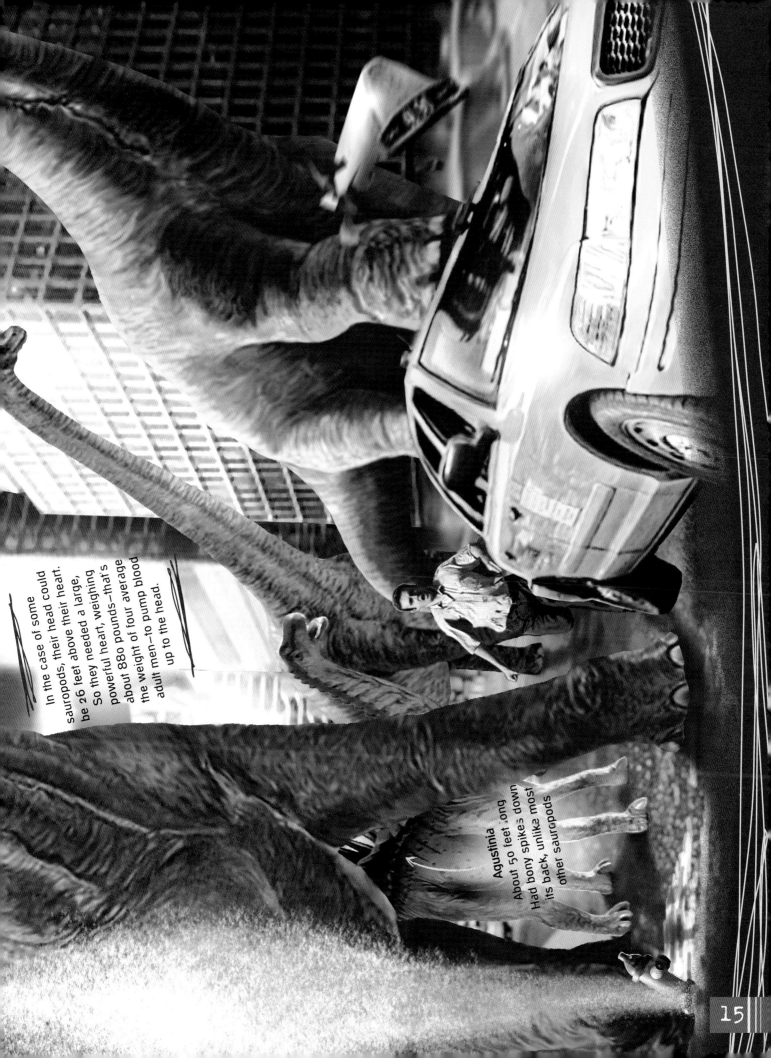

In the case of some sauropods, their head could be 26 feet above their heart. So they needed a large, powerful heart, weighing about 880 pounds—that's the weight of four average adult men—to pump blood up to the head.

Agustinia
About 50 feet long
Had bony spikes down its back, unlike most other sauropods

SMALL AND SAVAGE

MINI DINOSAURS

Some of the earliest dinosaurs were no larger than chickens! *Eoraptor* from the Triassic Period was about 3 feet long, and half of that was its tail. Some dinosaurs did evolve to be bigger and stronger, but others remained small. *Compsognathus*, from the Jurassic Period, was even smaller than *Eoraptor*.

Often running together in savage packs, the smaller hunters of the dinosaur world were deadly and terrifying. Armed with razor-sharp claws and teeth, they could run faster than anything else on Earth and bring down prey much larger than themselves with startling speed.

Velociraptor was one of the most intelligent dinosaurs. Its brain was relatively large in comparison to its body size.

Velociraptor was a smart turkey-sized predator. Although many images of this deadly hunter show it as a scaly reptile, we now know that it was actually covered in feathers and bird-like in appearance.

Velociraptor could run at speeds of up to 40 mph for short bursts.

Deadly battle

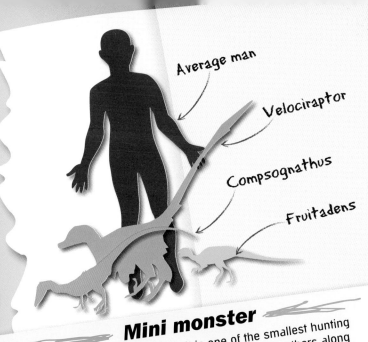

Average man
Velociraptor
Compsognathus
Fruitadens

Velociraptor was not afraid to attack larger animals. In 1971, fossils were found in Mongolia that showed a Velociraptor and a Protoceratops buried together. They had been fighting and the Protoceratops' beak had bitten deep into the Velociraptor, which had been attacking the Protoceratops with its claws. They may have died in a sudden sandstorm or when a sand dune collapsed.

Mini monster

Microraptor got its name because it is one of the smallest hunting dinosaurs known—only 15 inches long. It had flight feathers along both its arms and on its legs, so it probably climbed trees and glided from one to another. It may have pounced on prey by gliding onto it.

Dozy dino

The dinosaur with the shortest name is 2-foot-long Mei. This little hunting dinosaur lived about 130 million years ago in eastern Asia. Its name means "sleepy" because the first fossil found of this dinosaur is in the pose of a sleeping bird with its head tucked under its arm.

Insect picker

Six-foot-long Patagonykus had only one claw on each arm. Powerful muscles were attached to its arms and scientists think that Patagonykus may have used its claw to rip open termite mounds so that it could feed on the insects inside.

Sniff sniff

Byronosaurus had nasal bones that show it was very good at smelling things. Perhaps this five-foot-long dinosaur hunted at night and used its sense of smell to find food.

HIGH FLYER

One of the most successful agile early hunters was Coelophysis (see page 25). Scientists have found hundreds of fossils of this dinosaur buried together. The skull of one Coelophysis was taken into space in 1998 by the space shuttle Endeavour.

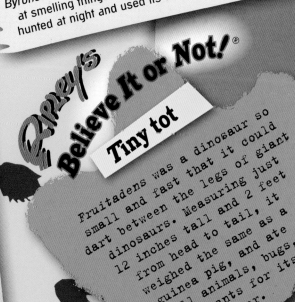

Ripley's Believe It or Not!®

Tiny tot

Fruitadens was a dinosaur so small and fast that it could dart between the legs of giant dinosaurs. Measuring just 12 inches tall and 2 feet from head to tail, it weighed the same as a guinea pig, and ate small animals, bugs, and plants for its dinner.

KNIGHTS IN ARMOR

POWERFUL PROTECTION

Encased in almost as much armor as a modern battle tank, and bristling with spikes, horns, and clubs, armored dinosaurs were awesome animals. Even the most ferocious hunter would think twice about launching an attack on them.

The bony armor that covered so many different types of dinosaurs—mainly the ankylosaur and stegosaur groups—was so protective that often the only way a predator could cause injury was by flipping the dinosaur over and exposing the soft belly. Judging by the size and shape of these beasts, that would not have been easy!

Scary tail

Ankylosaurus had a massive double-headed club on its tail. It may have used this to bash away at the armored backs of rivals in disputes over territory or status. This 20-foot-long chunky reptile was a herbivore and had to eat a huge amount of plant material to sustain itself, so its gut was very large. It probably had a fermentation chamber in its gut to aid in the digestion process. This offered another form of protection—enormous amounts of gas!

On a plate

All armored dinosaurs belong to one large group called the Thyreophora. Within the Thyreophora are the stegosaurs, ankylosaurs, scutellosaurs, and emausaurs. Many fossils of these dinosaurs are found upside down, as if a hunter had flipped them over to get to their less protected underbelly, and then used the shell as a plate from which to eat the juicy meat.

A LOT ON ITS PLATE

One of the earliest known armored dinosaurs, *Scutellosaurus* lived about 200 million years ago in the early Jurassic period. Only 4 feet long, it had more than 300 plates of bony armor—called scutes—set into its skin.

Blinking hard

Euoplocephalus was so heavily armored that even its eyelids were covered in bone. If provoked, all its armor may have filled with blood and turned pink.

twist it!

Yingshanosaurus was a stegosaur with a pair of huge spikes on its shoulders, each about 4 feet long. Unfortunately, the Chinese scientist who found the fossil has now lost it, so nobody can be certain what the dinosaur looked like.

Ankylosaurs and stegosaurs all belonged to the larger Thyreophora group of dinosaurs, all of which only ate plants. Thyreophora means "those who carry large shields."

However, with all that protection, there was little need to be able to run away from predators.

Given the weight of all that armor, ankylosaurs and stegosaurs were slow-moving creatures that walked on four legs.

KEEP OUT!

Sharp practice

Chialingosaurus was a smaller relative of *Stegosaurus*. It had bony plates on its neck and upper back, and spikes on its lower back and tail. As it was modestly sized, weighing just 500 pounds and measuring 13 feet in length, it might have been able to rear up on its hind legs and present a wall of spikes.

PRIZE FIGHTERS

POWER STRUGGLES

Take a ringside seat at this fight of the era. Charging toward each other at top speed, a pair of *Triceratops* clash with a resounding "thwack." Horns lock together, the ground vibrates, as each uses its strong shoulder muscles to try to wrestle the other backward into defeat. Battles between rival dinosaurs would have been terrifying.

It was not only meat-eating hunters that needed to fight. Many plant-eaters had to fight other dinosaurs of the same species over territory, food, or status. Some used displays of frills or feathers to scare off rivals, others had real weapons to use in their battles. Not every contest ended with serious injury, but some dinosaurs would have died in these fights.

YEE-HAA!

twist it!

Torosaurus had the largest frilled dinosaur skull, which was more than 8 feet long.

These dinosaurs would often bite each other's faces, often inflicting deep gashes, which have been found on some fossils.

Daspletosaurus was a slightly smaller relative of *Tyrannosaurus* that had a gaping mouth filled with huge sharp-tipped teeth. In battles, these dinosaurs would try to bite each other's faces, often inflicting deep gashes, which have been found on some fossils.

The family was given the name of pachycephalosaurs, which means "thick-headed-reptiles."

One family of dinosaurs had enormously thick bony domes on top of their skulls that were up to an incredible 8 inches thick. The family was given the name of pachycephalosaurs, which means "thick-headed-reptiles."

COME HERE AND SAY THAT!

Whip crack away

Seismosaurus and other sauropods had enormously long, whip-like tails that were controlled by powerful muscles. They could have used these tails to lash each other into defeat. Sauropods may also have used their necks to swing their heads and butt each other, in a similar way to giraffes today.

WHAT'S THE POINT?

Stegosaur tails all had a tip armed with long, sharp spikes called a "thagomizer." This unusual name was originally part of a joke in a 1982 cartoon by Gary Larson in which an unfortunate caveman called Thag has been killed by such a weapon. It is now used as an official term by paleontologists worldwide!

Triceratops means "three-horned face."

One of the most recognizable of all the dinosaurs, Triceratops was a plant-eating whopper that stood up to 10 feet tall and 30 feet in length. Its enormous skull could be one third the length of its body and its famous horns were probably used in mating rituals as well as for defense.

`Triceratops had no front teeth, so its mouth looked like a turtle's beak.`

BIG
WORD ALERT

PALEOICHNOLOGIST
A scientist who studies fossils of things left behind by animals, such as footprints and nests.

FINDING YOUR FEET

FEROCIOUS FOOTWEAR

Equipped with vicious claws, curving talons, or ponderous pads, dinosaur feet came in a variety of shapes and sizes. The design of their feet and legs was essential to the dinosaurs' success and made them the rulers of the world.

Dinosaur legs were positioned directly under their bodies, so the weight of the animal rested on the bones. In other reptiles, the legs splayed sideways, so the animal used more energy to work its muscles to lift its body off the ground. This meant that dinosaurs could move more efficiently than other animals when looking for food or escaping from danger, and this was enough to give them control of the Earth.

Big foot!

The feet of the biggest dinosaurs needed to be absolutely huge to support their massive weight. This scaled-down drawing shows how they compared to creatures of today.

Biggest dinosaur print found 57 inches

Tiger 9 inches

Elephant 19 inches

Domestic cat 1½ inches

That's gotta hurt
The thumb of the plant-eater Iguanodon took the form of a stout, very sharp spike. It may have been used in fights between rival Iguanodon.

Gone fishing
The front foot of Baryonyx carried a huge, curved claw. This may have been used to help the dinosaur catch fish from rivers or lakes.

The sauropod group of giant dinosaurs was named because of the arrangement of the bones inside their feet. "Sauropod" means "lizard foot."

Take cover!

Imagine this huge claw bearing down on your flesh. It sat, ready to rip, on the hind leg of Deinonychus. Only when the fossils of this dinosaur were discovered in the 1960s did scientists wise up to the fact that some dinosaurs had been fast, agile, and lethal. Before this, they thought dinosaurs had all been slow, lumbering beasts.

Claws call

The hind legs of **Allosaurus** and some other hunters carried three large claws, which were connected to powerful muscles. These may have been used to kick victims to death.

No escape

The gigantic, grasping hands of **Deinocheirus** were tipped with terrible 10-inch-long claws. On the end of 8-foot-long forelimbs, they were the ultimate far-reaching weapon.

Utterly useless

The front legs of **Tyrannosaurus** were so small that they could reach neither the ground nor the mouth. They could not even have been used to scratch itches.

Some dinosaurs had feet or claws designed for very specific purposes. Others, such as the mighty *Tyrannosaurus*, had powerful hind legs but surprisingly useless front legs.

ARMED TO THE TEETH

Open Mouths

Sharper than a steak knife and bigger than a dagger, the teeth of the immense hunter dinosaurs were ferocious weapons. Other dinosaurs had broad, flat teeth that were able to crush bones to powder. Plant-eaters had teeth designed for slicing, chopping, and grinding.

We can use fossilized teeth to discover what sort of food a dinosaur ate. If the jaws are found intact, they can show how the teeth were used when the dinosaur was feeding. Dinosaur teeth can also show who ate who in the dinosaur world. Scientists have found marks that match the teeth of a Tyrannosaurus on the bones of a Triceratops. And the broken off tip of an Allosaurus tooth has been found stuck in a sauropod bone.

Your point is?

One of the largest dinosaur teeth ever discovered was 11 inches long. It was found in North America and had a sharp point as it came from a meat-eater. Because the tooth was found on its own, nobody can be certain what type of dinosaur it came from.

LARGEST DINOSAUR TOOTH EVER FOUND

LARGE MEGALOSAURUS TOOTH

SMALL MEGALOSAURUS TOOTH

LION TOOTH

SMALL TYRANNOSAURUS TOOTH

HUMAN INCISOR

TRODON TOOTH

ALL TEETH ACTUAL SIZE

Tusk force

Heterodontosaurus had two pairs of long, sharp tusks near the front of its mouth, and smaller, grinding teeth at the rear of the jaws. It is thought that were used the tusks to dig up roots that were then chewed by the rear teeth.

Toothless

The fast-running ornithomimid dinosaurs had no teeth at all! Instead they had a beak, like that of a modern bird. It is thought that they ate lizards, beetles, and small animals.

Duck!

Gryposaurus had a giant, duck-like bill packed with hundreds of teeth. The 30-foot-long plant-eater had 300 teeth inside its beak, with a further 500 in its jaw ready to grow as replacements.

twist it!

Tyrannosaurus had teeth up to 12 inches long. Each tooth was narrow and edged with serrations that would have torn through flesh like a meat knife.

The largest dinosaur tooth found still in its owner's jaws belonged to a Daspletosaurus. The tooth was 8.6 inches long and 1.2 inches wide. Slightly curved and found at the front of the mouth, it was probably used to tear lumps of meat from a victim.

Hadrosaurs had massive rows of grinding teeth in their jaws to chew the tough plants that they ate. On average, each hadrosaur had about 4,000 teeth in its jaws.

The huge sauropod Supersaurus was one of the largest dinosaurs ever, but it had very small teeth. The adult animal was about 105 feet long, but each tiny tooth was only 1¼ inches long. That's like an adult human having teeth no thicker than a grain of rice.

SMILE PLEASE

Jagged edge

Coelophysis was one of the earliest dinosaurs and lived in the late Triassic period. It was an excellent hunter that could run fast and dart from side to side. Its sharp, curved, jagged teeth were perfect for gripping and eating small animals.

ON THE MENU

Gobbling up everything in sight, the giant dinosaurs stomped across the world consuming enormous amounts of food. They then deposited great big, stinking droppings behind them.

It is very difficult for scientists to estimate just how much different dinosaurs ate. The amount eaten would depend on the nutritional value of the food available, how efficient the dinosaur's body was at digesting the food, and how active they were. Fortunately, some dinosaur droppings have been fossilized and can be studied. They are known as coprolites.

Little taste

The alvarezsaurid family of dinosaurs may have eaten termites, ants, and other insects. They would have needed to eat several thousand every day.

Spinosaurus was a large deadly meat-eater that grew up to 60 feet in length and hunted alone. It had a preference for enormous fish and delicious fleshy chunks that it tore from the flanks of big dinosaurs with its crocodile-like jaws.

How rude!

Some animals regurgitated and spat out indigestible parts of food that they ate. Hunters may have eaten small animals whole, then spat out the bones. When these items are found as fossils they are known as "regurgitaliths."

CARNIVORE CUISINE

COCKTAIL OF THE HOUR
Swamp water at sundown

STARTER
Mixed mammal salad drizzled with blood

TODAY'S CATCH
Sea-trawled Elasmosaurus neck fillets, on a bed of volcanic ash

MAIN COURSE
Sauropod steak topped with an Oviraptor egg

DESSERT
Fried dragonflies with termite sauce

GOING VEGGIE

APERITIF
Freshly squeezed moss juice, served with pine pretzels

SOUP OF THE SEASON
Sun-roasted fern

MAIN COURSE
Fungal flambée, sulfur-smoked cycad cones, with a side order of tossed horsetails

DESSERT
Stripped twig roulade with magnolia flower garnish

Stones will be provided for swallowing and aiding digestion

What tickled the fancy of Stegosaurus were ferns, mosses, cycads, and baby evergreen trees. Good job, its neck was too short to reach any tall plants. These were nutritiously poor plants so Stegosaurus would have had to spend all day grazing in order to get enough nutrients to survive.

Puzzling flavor
Monkey puzzle trees evolved about the same time as the earliest plant-eating dinosaurs. They produce a fruit about the size of a football that is filled with tasty, nutritious seeds.

A pile of dinosaur dung 130 million years old was sold at a New York auction for $960 in April 2008. The fossilized dung, from the Jurassic period, was bought by Steve Tsengas of Fairport Harbor, Ohio.

Christmas lunch
The Picea spruce tree evolved about 100 million years ago and was probably a favorite food of the crested hadrosaur dinosaurs. It is still around today, but is better known as the Christmas tree.

Poo goes there?

Coprolites from many different dinosaur species have been found, but scientists find it very difficult to work out which dinosaur the poo originally came from, unless the coprolite was found inside a particular dinosaur's skeleton.

A street in the town of Felixstowe in England is called Coprolite Street!

COPROLITE

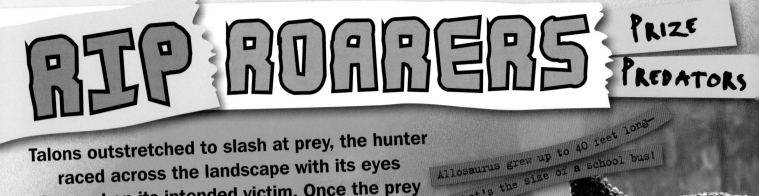

Talons outstretched to slash at prey, the hunter raced across the landscape with its eyes focused on its intended victim. Once the prey was reached, a rip with the claws brought it down, after which it was quickly killed. Then the great teeth began to tear into the flesh.

Allosaurus grew up to 40 feet long— that's the size of a school bus!

Some of the hunting dinosaurs combined large size and immense strength with the ability to run quickly and change direction with extreme agility. They had long hind legs, powered by strong leg and hip muscles, as well as large, curved claws on their small front legs.

This baby sauropod didn't stand much chance against these lethal predators.

BIG WORD ALERT

PREY
An animal that is hunted and killed by another animal for food.

JURASSIC LUNCH

This mighty mean *Allosaurus* doesn't look like he wants to share his lunch with the group of *Ceratosaurus* that have joined him in the late Jurassic forests of North America. Although *Allosaurus* hunted large plant-eating dinosaurs, such as the sauropod here, scientists think it may also have preyed on other predators, including *Ceratosaurus*—so these guys had better watch out!

RUUUUN!

More than 50 Allosaurus skeletons have been found–this is one of the highest numbers of fossil skeletons for any Jurassic dinosaur. About 70 percent of all big dinosaur hunters in North America 155 million years ago are believed to have been Allosaurus.

The hunter Saurophaganax is the state mascot of Oklahoma, where it was found. It was similar to Allosaurus, but even bigger.

Dinosaur footprints found at Glen Rose in Texas show a pack of four Acrocanthosaurus hunters stalking a herd of sauropods. There is even a track indicating that one of the hunters kicked at a prey with its hind leg.

A piece of fossilized skin from the hunter Carnotaurus shows that it had round, pebble-like scales interspersed with bony cones on its body.

TWIST it!

With razor-sharp teeth and horns, Ceratosaurus was just as scary as its deadly rival.

Ceratosaurus had a horn on the end of its nose and two smaller ones above its eyes. It grew to be 18 feet long and had a flexible tail that it could lash about.

BEAUTY AND THE BEASTS

It is safer for any animal to frighten off a rival or an attacker, rather than to fight. Even a strong beast might get hurt in a battle. By looking as big and as tough as possible, a dinosaur could frighten off a predator or challenge a rival of the same species.

Some dinosaurs were real show-offs, sporting wonderful, colorful plates, gigantic head crests, and multicolored tails. But these flourishes weren't just for fun. Dazzling dinosaurs wanted to bully and intimidate other animals, to protect themselves, get food, or attract a mate.

Moody Beast

The large bone plates on the back of *Stegosaurus* were covered in skin carrying large numbers of blood vessels. It is thought that the *Stegosaurus* could have changed the colors of the large plates to show what kind of mood it was in.

Twin Peak

Dilophosaurus was a 20-foot-long hunter that lived in North America about 190 million years ago. On top of its head the dinosaur had twin crests of paper-thin bone. These may have been brightly colored to act as signaling devices.

FAN TAIL

Nomingia had a flesh-covered bone protrusion on the end of its tail, just like that of a modern peacock. Scientists think that it had a large fan of brightly colored feathers that it could lift up and wave around in a threatening manner.

CROWNING GLORY

Styracosaurus, a large plant-eater that lived in the Cretaceous period, had a massive six-spiked frill projecting from the back of its skull, which might have been used in mating rituals and for scaring off rivals. These rivals could have included the mighty meat-eaters *Albertosaurus* and *Daspletosaurus*, who were around at the same time as *Styracosaurus*.

FLAG WAVERS

Several types of hadrosaur, such as this *Parasaurolophus*, had bone crests that pointed back from their heads. Some think that flaps of brightly colored skin connected the crest to the neck. By waggling its head, the dinosaur could wave these flaps as if they were flags.

Fancy Flyers

Some scientists think that the wings of pterosaurs may have been brightly colored. Reptile skin can take on shades of red, blue, or green, so the wings may have been as showy as those of modern parrots.

Boat or Dinosaur?

Spinosaurus (see page 26) had a sail of skin about 5 feet tall along its back. The dinosaur could have turned sideways to face a rival, flashing its brightly colored sail to make itself look as big as possible.

Big Head

Torosaurus had the largest skull of any land animal that ever lived. It was over 8 feet long, and most of the skin covering it was made up of a neck frill, which would have been brightly colored.

ON THE MOVE

HERDS AND MIGRATION

Plodding along in vast herds, scampering in the undergrowth alone, or waiting in ambush for a victim, dinosaurs were active animals leading dangerous lives in hostile places.

All dinosaurs had to find food, escape enemies, seek shelter from weather, and find mates. Most did not live alone, but moved about their environment in different ways. Some lived in huge herds, such as the duck-billed dinosaur *Maiasaura*, whose fossils have been found in groups of about 10,000 animals. Others, like *Deinonychus* and *Velociraptor*, may have hunted in deadly packs, attacking even gigantic sauropods. Family groups were common, among *Centrosaurus* for example, while *Allosaurus* and other species may have lived solitary lives for much of the time.

WALL WALKING

Near Sucre, Bolivia, a vertical wall of limestone contains over 5,000 fossilized footprints left by some 250 dinosaurs.

The footprints were left in the mud around the edge of a lake about 70 million years ago.

Over time, the mud turned to rock, which was then twisted upright as the Andes mountains formed.

Now it looks as though the dinosaurs were walking up a wall.

Herd this?

About 68 million years ago, dozens of *Centrosaurus* were drowned trying to cross a flooded river. The bodies of the drowned herd were covered by mud and later became fossils. The archeologists who discovered the fossils, at Alberta's Dinosaur Provincial Park in Canada, found the remains of the dinosaurs spread over an area about the size of a football field.

LIFE AS THEY KNEW IT

A large number of Triassic plant-eater *Plateosaurus* died crossing a desert that existed around what is now Trossingen, Germany. They were probably migrating from one food-rich area to another when they died.

Muttaburrasaurus is thought to have migrated 500 miles between its winter and summer grazing lands, in modern-day Australia.

In 2008, more than 1,000 dinosaur footprints were found on a ¾-acre site on the border of Utah and Arizona. Around 190 million years ago the area would have been a welcome watery oasis among hot, windswept sand dunes.

¡TI TSIM 9

Baby Comes Too

A set of fossil footprints found at Culpeper, Virginia, showed a number of huge sauropods walking in a small group. The adults were on the outside of the group and the young on the inside. It seems the adults were protecting the young from some threat.

Death by footprint

About 160 million years ago, a huge sauropod walked across a swamp in China. Lots of little Limusaurus, leaving footprints 6 feet deep. Lots of smaller dinosaurs, couldn't climb including Limusaurus, couldn't climb out, and died. Nine footprints, and fossils were found in one alone.

BIG WORD ALERT

MIGRATE
To move regularly between two or more different places, either to find food or to find safe places to bring up young.

33

STOP THAT DINOSAUR!

BUILT FOR SPEED

Dinosaurs were not all lumbering beasts that just plodded around their world. The swiftest of the dinosaurs could give the cheetahs and antelopes of today a run for their money. With pounding feet and awesome power, running dinosaurs could disappear into the distance in seconds.

Speed is useful for any animal, whether it's trying to catch prey or escape from a hunter. Most swift animals live on open plains with few hiding places, so they need to move quickly. Fast dinosaurs probably lived in dry, open areas with no trees and little vegetation

The fastest dinosaurs were the ornithomimosaurs, such as 12-foot-long *Dromiceiomimus*.

No way!

At this site near Cameron, Arizona, one man tries unsuccessfully to match the fossilized stride of a dinosaur predator that was as fast as an Olympic athlete.

LONG-LEGS

The ornithomimosaurs were large ostrich-like creatures, some of which ate meat.

Speed check

Cheetah
60 mph

Dromiceiomimus
50 mph

Tyrannosaurus
25 mph

No escaping

Speedy *Velociraptor* lived in Asia about 70 million years ago. It could run fast, and could whip its stiff tail from side to side to help it change direction when running at full speed.

Dromiceiomimus lived in North America about 80 million years ago.

Scientists think *Dromiceiomimus* could reach speeds of 50 mph.

Diplodocus was so heavy it could probably lift just one foot at a time.

Sprinter
Usain Bolt
23.35 mph

Elephant
15 mph

Mouse 7.5 mph

Diplodocus 5 mph

BIG MAMA
Newborns

All dinosaurs laid eggs, but working out their nesting behavior is very difficult. Scientists need to find fossils of a dinosaur's nests, eggs, and young to study, and, even then, it can be hard to piece together the mother's behavior.

Some dinosaurs built very carefully constructed nests in which to lay their eggs, and would have worked hard to find the ideal spot. Once the eggs were laid, some mothers would have guarded them against dangers, fed the babies when they hatched, and may even have looked after their young for months or years to come. Others walked away and let the hatchlings take their chances.

Giant egg nest

Seen here with an ordinary-sized chicken's egg, this is a nest of fossilized dinosaur eggs that was found in France. It isn't known which dinosaurs the eggs belonged to, but it looks like it must have been a lot bigger than a chicken!

Dinosaur auction

A nest of dinosaur eggs dating back 65 million years was sold at auction in Los Angeles in 2006 for $420,000. The nest, which was discovered in southern China in 1984, held 22 broken eggs, with some of the tiny unhatched dinosaurs clearly visible curled up inside. It was arranged in a circular pattern with the eggs placed along the edge. Scientists think it belonged to an oviraptor.

BIG WORD ALERT

INCUBATE
To keep eggs warm while the babies develop inside.

Baby dinosaurs grew very quickly and in some cases increased in size 16,000 times before reaching adulthood.

Triceratops laid its eggs in a spiral, Maiasaura in a circle. Sauropods left them in a row, as though the dinosaur laid them as she walked.

The smallest dinosaur eggs were about 1 inch across. They came from the small plant-eater Mussaurus.

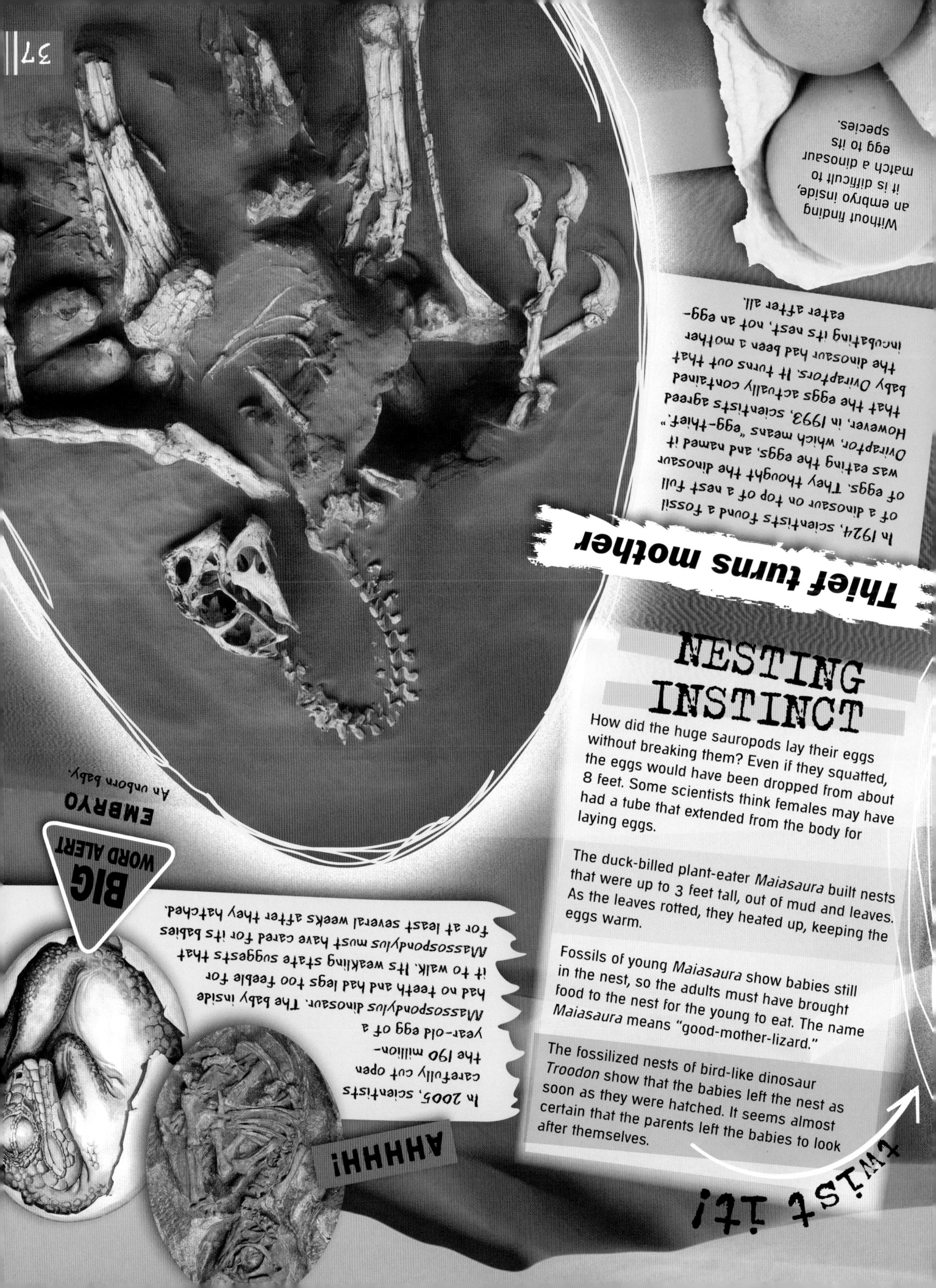

Without finding an embryo inside, it is difficult to match a dinosaur egg to its species.

In 1924, scientists found a fossil of a dinosaur on top of a nest full of eggs. They thought the dinosaur was eating the eggs, and named it Oviraptor, which means "egg-thief." However, in 1993, scientists agreed that the eggs actually contained baby Oviraptors. It turns out that the dinosaur had been a mother incubating its nest, not an egg-eater after all.

NESTING INSTINCT

How did the huge sauropods lay their eggs without breaking them? Even if they squatted, the eggs would have been dropped from about 8 feet. Some scientists think females may have had a tube that extended from the body for laying eggs.

The duck-billed plant-eater *Maiasaura* built nests that were up to 3 feet tall, out of mud and leaves. As the leaves rotted, they heated up, keeping the eggs warm.

Fossils of young *Maiasaura* show babies still in the nest, so the adults must have brought food to the nest for the young to eat. The name *Maiasaura* means "good-mother-lizard."

The fossilized nests of bird-like dinosaur *Troodon* show that the babies left the nest as soon as they were hatched. It seems almost certain that the parents left the babies to look after themselves.

twist it!

EMBRYO
An unborn baby.

BIG WORD ALERT

In 2005, scientists carefully cut open the 190-million-year-old egg of a *Massospondylus* dinosaur. The baby inside had no teeth and had legs too feeble for it to walk. Its weakling state suggests that *Massospondylus* must have cared for its babies for at least several weeks after they hatched.

AHHHH!

SKY PATROL

FLYING REPTILES AND BIRDS

The pterosaurs were a large group of flying reptiles that lived at the same time as the dinosaurs. They came in all shapes and sizes, ranging from gigantic gliders to small, agile flappers.

About 150 million years ago, the first birds evolved and began to take to the air. They gradually replaced the pterosaurs as the most important flying creatures, until only a few pterosaurs were left alive by the time of the great extinction 65 million years ago.

Soaring high above the ground, these flying reptiles twitched their great wings to swoop in a giant circle through the sky. Scanning the ground for the carcasses of a dead dinosaur, the pterosaurs sniffed the air for the tell-tale stink of rotting flesh.

The modern-day bat is the only mammal around today that is capable of sustained flight, and it's wings share many of the characteristics of a pterosaur wing.

Bats' wings are made from a fine membrane that connects their body to their arms and their long spread-out fingers. Pterosaur wings were made of a tough skin, but were attached to their bodies, arms, and fingers in a similar way. Birds, on the other hand, fly by using a row of feathers attached to each of their arms.

The pterosaur Pterodaustro had over a thousand bristle-like teeth in its jaws—about 62 per inch. It used these to filter tiny food particles from water.

These *Pteranodon* pterosaurs had huge, toothless bills, with which they caught their fish dinners, and wingspans of up to 30 feet.

Feathered friends

The fossil of a strange, feathered dinosaur from the middle to late Jurassic period—just before birds evolved—has been discovered in China. The pigeon-like creature, called Epidexipteryx, had four long ribbon-like tail feathers, which were probably used for display, but had no flight feathers. This fossil suggests that feathers were probably used for decoration millions of years before they were modified for flight.

Ripley's Believe It or Not!®

Giant glider

One of the largest of the pterosaurs was Quetzalcoatlus, which lived in North America about 72 million years ago. It had a wingspan of 36 feet—that's the same as some small aircraft.

One of the early birds

Confuciusornis was a primitive bird that lived about 120 million years ago in eastern Asia. It was about the size of a modern crow and had long tail feathers that ended in wide flags. Its fossils provide evidence of a strong link between dinosaurs and birds.

The smallest known pterosaur was Nemicolopterus, which lived in forests about in eastern years ago 120 million years ago. It was about the size of a modern blackbird with a wingspan of just 9 inches.

WILD WATERS

Fossils of ichthyosaurs sometimes contain round, black pebbles near the rear of the body. It is thought that these are fossilized droppings and they are colored black by the ink found in the squid that the ichthyosaurs ate.

HELP!

The dinosaurs also shared their world with several groups of water-dwelling reptiles, some of which were almost as big as them. These hungry sea giants powered their way through the waves snapping up fish, squid, ammonites, and other creatures in their tooth-fringed jaws. Some could even reach up into the air to grab flying pterosaurs on the wing.

Sea-going reptiles from the Mesozoic era included placodonts, ichthyosaurs, mosasaurs, plesiosaurs, and turtles. Some of these large water-dwelling reptiles died out before the dinosaurs did, others became extinct at the same time. There was one exception that lives on today: the turtles.

Living fossil?

A modern-day frill shark was found by a fisherman in Numazu, Japan, in 2007. Rarely seen out of its depth of 2,000 feet, this ancient-looking creature's body has many similarities to fossils of sharks that lived 350 million years ago.

Anyone for a swim?

A giant fossil sea monster found in the Arctic in 2008 had a bite that would have been able to crush a car. The marine reptile, which patrolled the oceans some 147 million years ago, measured 50 feet long and had a bite force of around 35,000 pounds.

Ripley's Believe It or Not!®

Big flipper

The fossils of the giant sea turtle *Archelon* date to around 75–65 million years ago, when a shallow sea covered most of North America. The largest specimen ever found is 13½ feet long and 16 feet wide from flipper to flipper.

The plesiosaurs were a group of sea reptiles with stout bodies and four powerful flippers. They flapped their flippers in a similar way to how birds' wings work. Pliosaurs were massive plesiosaurs with short, powerful necks and sharp teeth. Some were more than 35 feet long and might have been able to rear up to catch passing pterosaurs or birds.

Supersize!

The biggest ichthyosaur was *Shonisaurus*, which grew more than 70 feet long. Scientists found the fossils of 37 of these monsters in one small area in Nevada. Perhaps a family group had become stuck on a prehistoric beach and died.

The 45-foot-long plesiosaur *Elasmosaurus* had more bones in its neck than any other animal that has ever lived—72 in all.

Amazingly, no complete fossil has been found that is as big as the blue whale that lives on Earth with us today.

Killer Whale – 25 feet

Blue Whale – 100 feet

Elasmosaurus – 45 feet

Shonisaurus – 70 feet

Human!

DINO TIMES

MASSIVE METEORITE HITS EARTH!

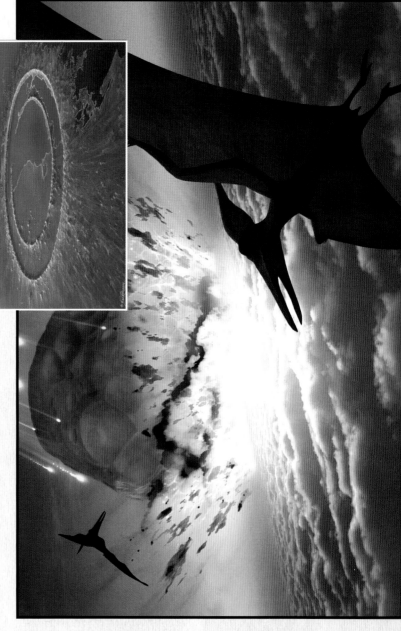

Scientists are agreed. Our planet has suffered a catastrophic meteorite hit in the Gulf of Mexico. Although reports are sketchy, as there is no sign of life in the immediate area, news is filtering through that the asteroid was about 6 miles wide and slammed into Earth at 43,000 miles per hour.

Reports suggest that, in just 30 seconds, the meteorite drilled a crater in Chicxulub, on the Yucatán Peninsula in Mexico, that was 24 miles deep and 125 miles wide. The meteorite collision has been compared to a blast from 100 megatons of high explosives.

Where is the sun?

Dust thrown up from the meteorite impact is starting to block out sunlight. As a result, in many parts of the world, temperatures have dropped. Our dinosaur in the field has seen trees that are wilting and dying from lack of light. A *Triceratops* that depends on foliage for food moans, "We always have to eat a lot and now there's just not enough to go round."

Sightings of *Tyrannosaurus* and other meat-lovers gorging on weakened herbivores are becoming increasingly rare. "When the dark days first set in, forests began to die and dying herbivores were everywhere. Frankly, times were good," explains one. "But now their carcasses are starting to go off and we're panicking that fresh meat could be a thing of the past."

Hard to Breathe

Air quality is poor, as poisonous volcanic gases are becoming trapped under the dust clouds and ash continues to rain down. In some areas, gases have been acting like a lid on the world's atmosphere and have trapped in heat from volcanic activity. Rivers have dried and deserts are growing—all presenting more problems for plants and animals.

WEATHER WARNING!

Tsunamis, earthquakes, and hurricane winds imminent.

Today's Horoscope

Those born in the Mesozoic era will be confronting new challenges. Hold tight on booking next year's vacation.

JOKE OF THE DAY

What comes after extinction?
Y-stinction, of course!

Obituaries: Extinction has been announced of the following dinosaurs: Every single one.

DINO STATS

All the facts and figures on the main dinosaurs you'll find in this book.

KEY TO SYMBOLS

L = Length   **H** = Height   **W** = Weight

🌿 Herbivore (a plant-eating dinosaur)

⚫ Carnivore (a meat-eating dinosaur)

⚫🌿 Omnivore (a plant- and meat-eating dinosaur)

T = Triassic period

J = Jurassic period

C = Cretaceous period

AFROVENATOR
say *af-ro-vee-nay-tor*
"African hunter"
Type theropod
L 30 feet   **H** 10 feet   **W** 3,000 pounds
 C

AGUSTINIA
say *ah-gus-tin-ee-ah*
"for Agustin"
Type sauropod
L 50 feet   **H** 15 feet   **W** 20,000 pounds
 C

ALLOSAURUS
say *al-oh-saw-russ*
"different lizard"
Type theropod
L 40 feet   **H** 15 feet   **W** 6,600 pounds
⚫ **J**

ANKYLOSAURUS
say *an-key-low-saw-rus*
"fused lizard"
Type ankylosaur
L 20 feet   **H** 9 feet   **W** 8,000 pounds
 C

ARGENTINOSAURUS
say *are-jen-teen-owe-saw-rus*
"silver lizard"
Type sauropod
L 130 feet   **H** 35 feet   **W** 160,000 pounds
 C

BARYONYX
say *ba-ree-on-ix*
"heavy claw"
Type theropod
L 32 feet   **H** 15 feet   **W** 4,400 pounds
 C

BRACHIOSAURUS
say *brack-ee-oh-saw-rus*
"arm lizard"
Type sauropod
L 80 feet   **H** 42 feet   **W** 155,000 pounds
 J

CERATOSAURUS
say *see-rat-oh-saw-rus*
"horned lizard"
Type ceratosaur
L 18 feet   **H** 10 feet   **W** 3,000 pounds
⚫ **J**

CHIALINGOSAURUS
say *chee-ah-ling-oh-saw-rus*
"Chialing lizard"
Type stegosaur
L 13 feet   **H** 5 feet   **W** 500 pounds
 J

COELOPHYSIS
say *see-low-fy-sis*
"hollow form"
Type theropod
L 10 feet   **H** 3 feet   **W** 100 pounds
⚫ **T**

COMPSOGNATHUS
say *comp-sog-nay-thus*
"pretty jaw"
Type theropod
L 28 inches   **H** 10 inches   **W** 6 pounds
⚫ **J**

DEINOCHEIRUS
say *dine-oh-kir-us*
"terrible hand"
Type ornithomimosaur
L 23–38 feet   **H** 10 feet   **W** 20,000 pounds
 C

DEINONYCHUS
say *die-non-i-kuss*
"terrible claw"
Type dromeosaur
L 10 feet   **H** 5 feet   **W** 175 pounds
⚫ **C**

DIPLODOCUS
say *dee-plod-oh-cus*
"double-beam"
Type sauropod
L 90 feet   **H** 16 feet   **W** 27,000 pounds
 J

DROMICEIOMIMUS
say *droh-mee-see-oh-my-mus*
"emu mimic"
Type ornithomimosaur
L 12 feet   **H** 6 feet   **W** 250 pounds
 C

EUOPLOCEPHALUS
say *you-oh-plo-sef-ah-lus*
"well-armored head"
Type ankylosaur
L 23 feet   **H** 8 feet   **W** 4,000 pounds
 C

FRUITADENS
say *fruit-ah-denz*
"fruita tooth"
Type heterodontosaur
L 28 inches   **H** 12 inches   **W** 2 pounds
 J

GRYPOSAURUS
say *grip-oh-saw-us*
"hook-nosed lizard"
Type hadrosaur
L 30 feet   **H** 12–14 feet   **W** 6,000 pounds
 C

IGUANODON
say *ig-wah-no-don*
"iguana tooth"
Type iguanodont
L 30 feet   **H** 12 feet   **W** 9,900 pounds
 C

MAMENCHISAURUS
say *mah-men-chee-saw-rus*
"mamen lizard"
Type sauropod
L 75 feet   **H** 30 feet   **W** 30,000 pounds
 J

MASSOSPONDYLUS
say *mass-oh-spon-dye-luss*
"massive vertebra"
Type prosauropod
L 16 feet   **H** 6 feet   **W** 300 pounds
 J

NOMINGIA

say *no-ming-ee-uh*

"Nomingiin" (part of the Gobi desert)

Type oviraptor

L 6 feet   **H** 2½ feet   **W** 70 pounds

OVIRAPTOR

say *ov-ee-rap-tor*

"egg thief"

Type theropod

L 8 feet   **H** 3 feet   **W** 75 pounds

PROTOCERATOPS

say *pro-toe-sair-ah-tops*

"first horned face"

Type ceratopsian

L 8 feet   **H** 3 feet   **W** 900 pounds

SCIPIONYX

say *sip-ee-on-ix*

"scipio's claw"

Type theropod

L 6 feet   **H** 2½ feet   **W** 25 pounds

SCUTELLOSAURUS

say *skoo-tel-o-saw-us*

"little shield lizard"

Type thyreophora

L 4 feet   **H** 18 inches   **W** 25 pounds

SEISMOSAURUS

say *size-mow-saw-rus*

"earthquake lizard"

Type sauropod

L 130 feet   **H** 18 feet   **W** 66,000 pounds

SPINOSAURUS

say *spy-no-saw-rus*

"spiny lizard"

Type spinosaur

L 60 feet   **H** 22 feet   **W** 20,000 pounds

STEGOSAURUS

say *steg-oh-saw-rus*

"roofed lizard"

Type stegosaur

L 30 feet   **H** 9 feet   **W** 6,000 pounds

STYRACOSAURUS

say *sty-rak-o-saw-us*

"spiked lizard"

Type ceratopsian

L 18 feet   **H** 6 feet   **W** 6,500 pounds

TRICERATOPS

say *tyr-seer-ah-tops*

"three horned face"

Type ceratopsian

L 30 feet   **H** 10 feet   **W** 22,000 pounds

TYRANNOSAURUS

say *tie-ran-oh-saw-rus*

"tyrant lizard king"

Type tyrannosaur

L 40 feet   **H** 18 feet   **W** 14,000 pounds

VELOCIRAPTOR

say *vel-oh-see-rap-tor*

"speedy thief"

Type theropod

L 6 feet   **H** 3 feet   **W** 65 pounds

DINOSAUR FAMILY TREE

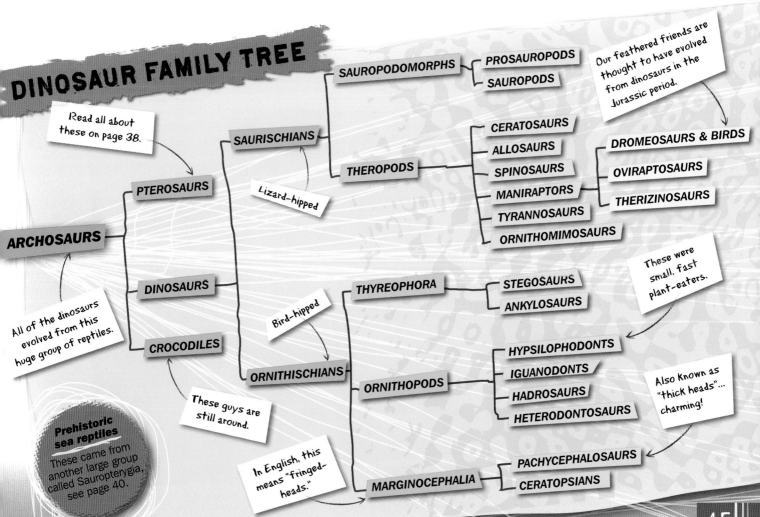

Our feathered friends are thought to have evolved from dinosaurs in the Jurassic period.

Read all about these on page 38.

ARCHOSAURS

PTEROSAURS

DINOSAURS

CROCODILES

SAURISCHIANS — Lizard-hipped

SAUROPODOMORPHS — PROSAUROPODS / SAUROPODS

THEROPODS — CERATOSAURS / ALLOSAURS / SPINOSAURS / MANIRAPTORS / TYRANNOSAURS / ORNITHOMIMOSAURS

MANIRAPTORS — DROMEOSAURS & BIRDS / OVIRAPTOSAURS / THERIZINOSAURS

ORNITHISCHIANS — Bird-hipped

THYREOPHORA — STEGOSAURS / ANKYLOSAURS

These were small, fast plant-eaters.

ORNITHOPODS — HYPSILOPHODONTS / IGUANODONTS / HADROSAURS / HETERODONTOSAURS

MARGINOCEPHALIA — PACHYCEPHALOSAURS / CERATOPSIANS

Also known as "thick heads"… charming!

In English, this means "fringed-heads."

These guys are still around.

All of the dinosaurs evolved from this huge group of reptiles.

Prehistoric sea reptiles
These came from another large group called Sauropterygia, see page 40.

INDEX

Bold numbers refer to main entries; numbers in *italic* refer to the illustrations

ACKNOWLEDGMENTS

COVER (dp) © zsollere – Fotolia.com, (r) Leonardo Meschini Advocate Art **2** (b) © Ralf Kraft – Fotolia.com; **2–3** © Robert King – Fotolia.com; **3** (t) © Fabian Kerbusch – iStock.com; **4** (b/l) © Sergey Drozdov – Fotolia.com; **5** (t/r) © Klaus Nilkens – iStock.com; **6** Mark Garlick/Science Photo Library; **6–7** © Metin Tolun – Fotolia.com; **7** (sp) © Alwyn Cooper – iStock.com, (t/l) © Bill May – iStock.com, (r) © Todd Harrison – iStock.com; **8** (l) © Ericos – Fotolia.com, (r) © Olga Orehkova-Sokolova – Fotolia.com; **8–9** (b) © zobeedy – Fotolia.com; **9** (t) © Metin Tolun – Fotolia.com, (t/r) Laurie O'keefe/Science Photo Library, (l) © Olga Orehkova-Sokolova – Fotolia.com, (r) © Ericos – Fotolia.com; **10** (t/l) © Didier Dutheil/Sygma/Corbis, (r) Photo courtesy of Charlie and Florence Magovern; **10–11** (c) © Metin Tolun – Fotolia.com; **11** (t/r) Reuters/STR New, (t) © Bill May – iStock.com, (b/r) © Didier Dutheil/Sygma/Corbis; **12** (b/l) Mikkel Juul Jensen/Bonnier Publications/Science Photo Library, (c) © Robert King – Fotolia.com, (t) © Fabian Kerbusch – iStock.com, (t/r) Eightfish; **13** (t) © Fabian Kerbusch – iStock.com, (t/r) © greenmedia – Fotolia.com, (c/r) © LianeM – Fotolia.com, (r) © Duey – Fotolia.com, (b/r) Reuters/Sergio Moraes, (sp) © Czardases – Fotolia.com; **14–15** Leonardo Meschini Advocate Art; **16** (sp) Roger Harris/Science Photo Library **17** (b/l) © Metin Tolun – Fotolia.com, (b/cl) © Bill May – iStock.com, (t) Christian Jegou Publiphoto Diffusion/Science Photo Library, (b) Reuters/STR New; **18** (t) De Agostini/Getty Images, (t/l) © Paul Moore – Fotolia.com, (b) © Metin Tolun – Fotolia.com, (b/r) Highlights for Children (OSF)/www.photolibrary.com; **18–19** (sp) © Ivan Bliznetsov – iStock.com, (r, l) © Steven van Soldt – iStock.com; **19** (t) Photoshot, (t/l) © Joonarkan – Fotolia.com, (c) © Sabina – Fotolia.com, (b) De Agostini/ Getty Images; **20–21** Leonardo Meschini Advocate Art; **21** (t/r) © Olga Orehkova-Sokolova – Fotolia.com; **22–23** Leonardo Meschini Advocate Art; **24** (sp) Colin Keates; **25** (t/l) © Michael S. Yamashita/Corbis, (t/r) Ken Lucas, (b) Dea Picture Library; **26** (c) © Ralf Kraft – Fotolia.com (b/l, t/r) © Serhiy Zavalnyuk – iStock.com, (b/r) © Little sisters – Fotolia.com; **26–27** © klikk – Fotolia.com; **27** (t/l) © Little sisters – Fotolia.com, (t/r) © Olga Orehkova-Sokolova – Fotolia.com, (b) Peter Menzel/Science Photo Library; **28–29** Leonardo Meschini Advocate Art; **30** (b/c) Leonardo Meschini Advocate Art, (b) © Metin Tolun – Fotolia.com; **30–31** © Petya Petrova – Fotolia.com; **31** (t/l) Jeffrey L. Osborn, (t, b) © Metin Tolun – Fotolia.com, (b/r) Joe Tucciarone/Science Photo Library; **32** (t/r) Nigel Tisdall/Rex Features; **32–33** (dp) © Louie Psihoyos/Science Faction/Corbis; **33** (r) Christian Darkin/Science Photo Library; **34** (l) © Louie Psihoyos/Science Faction/Corbis, (b/l, b/r) © zobeedy – Fotolia.com, (b/c) © N & B – Fotolia.com; **34–35** Leonardo Meschini Advocate Art; **35** (b/l) © Pawel Nowik – Fotolia.com, (b/c) © N & B – Fotolia.com, (b/cr) © a_elmo – Fotolia.com, (b/r) © zobeedy – Fotolia.com; **36** (t) © Louie Psihoyos/Science Faction/Corbis, (b/r) © Chris Hepburn – iStock.com; **36–37** (dp) © Vladimir Wrangel – Fotolia.com; **37** (t/r) Reuters/Ho New, (b) © Louie Psihoyos/Corbis; **38** (t/l) © Gijs Bekenkamp – iStock.com; **38–39** Jaime Chirinos/Science Photo Library; **39** (t/l) Joe Tucciarone/Science Photo Library, (t) © Hypergon – iStock.com, (t/r) Richard Bizley/Science Photo Library; **40** (c) Getty Images, (b) search4dinosaurs.com; **41** Reuters/Ho New; **42** (b/r) © Darren Hendley – iStock.com, (c/r) © nikzad khaledi – iStock.com, (t/l) D. Van Ravenswaay/Science Photo Library, (t) Mauricio Anton/Science Photo Library; **43** Mark Garlick/Science Photo Library

Key: t = top, b = bottom, c = center, l = left, r = right, sp = single page, dp = double page, bgd = background

All other photos are from Ripley's Entertainment Inc. All other artwork by Rocket Design (East Anglia) Ltd.

Every attempt has been made to acknowledge correctly and contact copyright holders and we apologize in advance for any unintentional errors or omissions, which will be corrected in future editions.